GAMBLER

by David Belbin

Series Editors: Steve Barlow and Steve Skidmore

Heinemann

Published by Heinemann Educational Publishers
Halley Court, Jordan Hill, Oxford OX2 8EJ
A division of Reed Educational and Professional Publishing Ltd

OXFORD MELBOURNE AUCKLAND
JOHANNESBURG BLANTYRE GABORONE
IBADAN PORTSMOUTH (NH) USA CHICAGO

First published 2002

06 05 04 03 02
10 9 8 7 6 5 4 3 2 1

ISBN 0 435 21417 9

Illustrations by Keith Page
Cover design by Shireen Nathoo Design
Designed and typeset by Artistix, Thame, Oxon
Printed and bound in Great Britain by Athenaeum Press Ltd

Tel: 01865 888058 www.heinemann.co.uk

Contents

Nobody wants to change schools at fifteen, but Johnny Todd didn't have a choice. His whole family had moved south for his dad's new job.

Johnny didn't like his new school much. He looked old for his age and boys were wary of him. The good-looking girls didn't seem to notice he was there. Whole days would go by when the only people who spoke to Johnny were teachers. Johnny only looked forward to one thing at school. Every lunch time, he played cards.

He'd found the game in his second week. It took place behind the workshops. Most of the kids who played were younger than Johnny. They didn't dare object when he joined the pontoon game. It was a bit sad, playing with younger kids, but it wasn't as though they were his friends. Hardly anybody even spoke, except to say 'twist', 'stick' or 'bust'.

Some days, Johnny won. Other days, he lost a little. It wasn't a very exciting game, but it was better than spending lunchtimes on his own.

One Friday, when Johnny had been at his new school for a month, a stranger joined the game. Johnny had seen this guy around, but had no idea who he was. The lad was stocky, with thick black hair and a single gold ear-stud. He hardly looked at his first card. Then he bet a quid. The usual limit was fifty pence, but the dealer said nothing. The dealer stuck on twenty.

The new player lost. On the next deal, he bet two quid. This time he won. On the next deal, he bet four quid and twisted twice. Johnny was sure he'd go bust, but the new player kept betting. Soon he had five cards.

The dealer played nervously. He twisted

on seventeen. He should have stuck then, but didn't. His next card was a ten. Bust. The new player had been in the game for two minutes and had already won five pounds.

He laid down his five-card trick and got up to go.

'Oh come on, Ace,' said the dealer. 'Give me a chance to win my money back.'

'If you insist,' the new player said. He looked like he couldn't care less.

This time, Ace bet five pounds without even looking at his first card. He twisted an ace and stuck. All eyes were on the dealer.

For his first card, the dealer turned over a ten. He twisted, and got a five. Taking a deep breath, the dealer twisted again. This time, he got a six.

'Pay pontoons and five-card tricks only,' he said.

Slowly smiling, Ace turned over his first card. It was a three. His hand was worth nothing.

'Easy come, easy go,' Ace said. He winked at Johnny, handed over the five pounds and left.

'Who was that guy?' Johnny asked.

'Ace Black,' the dealer said, as if Johnny should know. 'Haven't you heard of Vic Black?'

'The footballer?' Johnny asked. Vic Black was a big star for England, about ten years ago.

'That was his son,' the dealer told Johnny. 'People call him Ace because all he's interested in is playing cards.'

'Where does he play?' Johnny asked.

'There's a game at his house most lunchtimes,' the dealer told him.

'Maybe I could join in,' Johnny said.

'Doubt it,' the dealer told him. 'Most of the players are in the Sixth Form.'

'Ace doesn't look that old.'

'He's in Year Eleven.'

'Then why does he bother with this game?' Johnny wanted to know.

'He stops by now and then to wind us up,' the dealer replied. 'I think he just likes to bet.'

'Me too,' Johnny said, wondering how he could make Ace Black his friend.

CHAPTER 2

Johnny didn't see Ace again until half-term.
The footballer's son was walking down his
street. Seeing Johnny, Ace called him over.

'Weren't you in that blackjack game at
school?' he asked.

'Don't you mean pontoon?' Johnny said.

'Real gamblers call it blackjack,' Ace told
him. 'You were playing behind the
workshops, weren't you?'

'Yeah, that was me,' Johnny replied.

'Like a bet, do you?' Ace asked.

'It helps to pass the time,' said Johnny.

'You could find a better game,' Ace said.

'Where?'

'Round mine, tomorrow afternoon. You
know how to play poker?'

'Of course,' Johnny replied.

Ace gave him the address. 'Bring plenty of money,' he added.

Next day, Johnny turned up at Ace's house right on time. He was hoping to meet Ace's dad. However, there was no sign of the famous footballer.

'What does your dad do now?' he asked.

'As little as possible,' Ace told him. 'He opens supermarkets and does the match commentary on Sky Sports now and then.'

'Lucky him,' Johnny said.

'He's earned his luck,' Ace boasted. 'He was England's top scorer two seasons running.'

'Who else is playing?' Johnny asked.

'They'll be here soon,' Ace said. 'Are you sure you know the rules?'

'Run through them for me, would you?'

Ace took Johnny through the rules. You were dealt five cards and had to bet or fold. Then you could change any of your cards before the next round of betting. At the end, four of a kind beat everything except a running flush – five cards of the same suit, in order. Aces were high.

'The harder a hand is to get, the more it's worth,' Ace explained. 'A lot of it is just working out the maths.'

The other players arrived. Tom, Griff and Satnam were in the Sixth Form. Before an hour was up, Johnny had lost all his money to them.

'Want me to lend you some?' Ace offered.

'No thanks,' Johnny replied. *Neither a borrower nor a lender be*, his dad always said.

'What do you reckon then, lads?' Ace said to the others. 'Shall we let Johnny join the game?'

'Sure,' Satnam said. 'As long as he keeps losing.'

Everyone laughed at that.

'You're in,' Ace told Johnny at the door. 'We play every day except Friday. You did well. We've not had anyone from Year Ten before.'

'No one?' Johnny said, his chest swelling.

'Except for when I was in Year Ten, of course,' Ace said, cheerfully. 'See you.'

Mrs Black came home just as Johnny was leaving. She had been a beauty queen and worked as a model now. When Mrs Black smiled at Johnny, he felt like he'd won the lottery.

CHAPTER 3

On Monday, Johnny took a packed lunch to school and ate it at break. He didn't want to be late for the game. He got to Ace's place at ten past twelve. A tall lad was waiting outside.

'Who are you?' he asked Johnny.

'I'm a mate of Ace's,' Johnny explained. 'The others invited me to join the game.'

The tall lad didn't reply, for a BMW was drawing up in the drive. Ace's mum got out. She looked like she'd just had her hair done.

'Is Ace keeping you waiting, Darren?' Mrs Black asked. 'Come inside.'

Ace's mum gave Johnny and Darren a beer. There was no sign of Ace's dad.

'It must be weird, having a mum who looks so young,' Johnny said when she'd gone.

'She's not Ace's real mum,' Darren sneered. 'Vic Black dumped his first wife for her.'

'Oh!' Johnny felt stupid. Luckily, the others arrived a moment later. They settled down to a game. Johnny soon started losing. His money trickled away. Then, towards the end of lunchtime, he got a pair of jacks. He thought he was going to win, but Ace made a really high bet. He was bound to have something better, so Johnny threw his hand in.

Ace laughed as he took the pot. Then he showed his cards. He only had an ace high.

'Easy come, easy go,' said Johnny. He was cleaned out, and would have to use his post office money if he wanted to play again. But at least the other players had accepted him.

As he left, Mrs Black called, 'See you tomorrow, Johnny.' She'd remembered his name.

The next day, when Ace tried to bluff him, Johnny saw him, and won the pot.

He even managed a bluff of his own. He took two quid off Darren by pretending to have a full house – three of one kind and a pair of another.

By Thursday, Johnny had lost thirteen quid. At that rate, his savings would be gone in no time. But he was getting better. That night, he taped *Late Night Poker* on Channel Four. Over the weekend he watched it twice. He wanted to pick up as many tips as possible. The main thing, it seemed, was to keep your cool.

The following Monday there were only five of them in the game.

'Sorry lads,' Ace said. 'There's no beer in the house. Dad had a heavy weekend. He's still in bed, so we'd better keep the noise down.'

Everyone was serious about the game. This helped Johnny to concentrate. Early on, he got three tens. That was a good hand, but he played as though he wasn't sure of it.

Soon, it was just him and Darren. Darren raised him a pound. Johnny took a deep breath, then raised Darren by two pounds. Darren swore. He had to borrow the two pounds to see Johnny.

'Three tens,' Johnny said.

'Who let him play?' Darren demanded, tossing his pair of kings onto the floor. 'I'm off.'

'Don't worry about Darren,' Ace told Johnny as they walked back to school together. 'He'll be all right, as long as you don't beat him every day. Nobody likes to lose.'

'Most people lose, most days,' Johnny said.

'Not me,' Ace said. 'I'm always ahead.'

This wasn't true, Johnny knew. Yet Ace seemed to think it was, so Johnny said nothing.

CHAPTER 4

Next day, Johnny showed up at Ace's house on time, but the game was already under way. Some of the sixth formers had had a free period, Satnam told him. Vic Black had let them in early.

'Vic joined us for a couple of hands,' said Tom. 'He really likes his poker.'

'Where is Vic now?' Johnny asked. He was still hoping to meet the former England player.

'He'll be at the golf club,' Ace said. 'Dad more or less lives there.'

'How do you fancy a little late night poker?' Ace asked Johnny after the game.

'You mean the TV show?' Johnny asked.

'What TV show?' Ace said. 'No, this is here, next Saturday night.'

'Sure,' Johnny said. 'What time?'

'Ten. We play until the last man's standing.'

Johnny had a problem. He couldn't come home at whatever time he wanted. And he didn't live on an expensive estate near the school, like Ace. His house was a ten-minute taxi ride away. Still, he decided to chance his luck.

'Can I crash on a sofa afterwards?'

'Sure,' Ace said.

Johnny worried what his parents would say. But when he told them that he was staying overnight at Vic Black's house, they were really impressed. Dad even offered to give him a lift.

'Is Vic still married to that beauty queen?' Dad asked on the way there.

'Yeah, and she still looks fantastic.'

'Some people are born lucky,' Dad said.

CHAPTER 5

The big game started slowly. Nobody wanted to lose a lot early in the evening. Once you were out, you were out. Johnny played a steady game. He was watching how the others played.

Griff was reckless. Johnny could read him like a book. Tom played the way Johnny did. He was clever and careful. Darren drank too much. Satnam was a good player. Ace was better. He played like he knew what cards they had. Soon he was a little ahead.

Tom was the first to be knocked out.

'I'll stay and deal,' Tom said, as the front door opened. Ace's mum and dad had been at the golf club. From the hall, Johnny heard the voice of the former England striker.

'Sounds like the boys' card game is still going. Think I'll join them for a few hands.'

'And I think not,' said the former Miss England. She put her head around the door. 'Everything all right, boys?' she asked. 'We'll say goodnight, then. Don't make too much noise when you leave. You know what the neighbours are like.'

Johnny needed one more card to make a running flush. He said no to a third beer and raised the pot by two quid.

'You're bluffing,' Darren said, taking a new can of beer. 'Raise you five pounds.'

Johnny matched Darren's bet. There were only two of them left in the hand. Johnny changed one card, Darren two. Johnny needed a four of spades to make a running flush, Ace high. The odds were slim. He wondered what Darren had.

Johnny turned over his new card. It was a four of hearts. He had a run, but lots of things could beat that. Darren grinned. Johnny tried to keep a straight face. It was Darren's turn to bet.

'All in,' Darren said, pushing his pile of money into the centre of the table. There was just under ten pounds. Darren dropped his cards face down and poured himself some more beer. Johnny didn't know what to do. He had more money than Darren, but not much more. He reckoned his chances were fifty-fifty. It all depended on whether Darren was bluffing.

Everybody was looking at Johnny, waiting for his decision. Darren gulped down some more beer. There were beads of sweat on his forehead. Instinct told Johnny that the older boy was bluffing. He took a deep breath.

'See you,' he said.

Instead of showing his cards, Darren shouted. 'You looked at my cards as I put them down!'

'That's a stupid lie,' Johnny said, shocked.

'I saw you staring! You know it's a bluff.'

The other boys looked on warily. Johnny wondered how drunk Darren was.

'I couldn't see your cards,' he said. 'Even if I had, it would be your fault. You dropped them on the table like you didn't care who saw them.'

Johnny hoped that Ace would settle this. But Darren was older than Ace, and bigger.

'Why don't we get this over with?' Satnam said mildly. 'Go on, both show your cards.'

Johnny laid out his run. Darren only had a pair. The older boy got up angrily.

'You knew what I had. Cheat!'

He stormed out of the room. Darren's game was over.

Griff frowned. 'He's not normally such a bad loser,' he told Johnny. 'It's the drink. *Did* you see his cards?'

'No, I didn't!' Johnny insisted.

The incident left a bad taste. Griff was soon out. Satnam followed. At four in the morning, only Ace and Johnny were left playing.

'Last man standing,' Ace reminded Johnny. 'But I'm whacked. Want to hit the sack?'

'Definitely,' Johnny said. 'You're a mate.'

'One thing,' Ace said, as he unfolded the sofa bed. 'If the others ask, I cleaned you out.'

'I lost every penny,' Johnny agreed with a grin. 'You're the champion.'

'Always,' Ace said, patting Johnny on the back before going up to bed.

CHAPTER 6

After that Saturday night, Johnny's confidence was high. The next week, he came out ahead in every game. Playing poker paid like having a part-time job. Johnny found himself dreaming about poker. He learnt all the odds. Whatever the hand, he could work out what chance he had to win. There was luck involved, but not a lot.

Johnny was having such a good time, he hardly noticed that there were fewer players than usual. Darren didn't show up once. Then, one morning break, Ace came to see him.

'Better if you don't play today, mate.'

'What's the problem?' Johnny asked.

'People don't like being beaten by someone three years younger than them,' Ace said.

'I can lose more hands,' Johnny offered.

'No. They've seen how sharp you are with cards. They'd think you were up to something.'

'There's got to be a way!' Johnny was desperate. He'd be lost without poker.

'Forget it,' Ace said. 'I'm sorry, mate.'

'What am I going to do?' Johnny asked.

'I'll tell you what I used to do, before I started playing at home,' Ace said. 'You know that game behind the workshops? I started it.'

'But it's only blackjack. That's kids' stuff.'

'So teach them to play poker,' Ace urged.

Johnny realised that he didn't have a choice. He had to play cards. So, the next day, he returned to the game behind the workshops.

'This is boring,' he said, after two days of pontoon. 'Anyone fancy playing poker?'

Patiently, he taught the younger kids how to play. It was better than nothing. And, as the weather got warmer, the poker game got really popular. Year Eleven lads joined in. The younger kids took it in turns to act as look-out.

When the Sixth Form exams were on, Ace came by, looking for a game.

Within a week, he was coming every day. It was good to see him. In this game, Ace didn't do better than Johnny.

'You can start coming back to mine next year,' Ace said at the end of school.

'I'm doing pretty well here,' Johnny said.

'It's kids' stuff,' Ace said. 'Top bet's only a quid! You like to gamble higher. Let's cut.'

'What's the bet?' Johnny asked, curious.

'Aces high. A tenner for the highest card.'

'You're on.' Johnny cut the pack and drew the ace of spades. A winner.

'I can't pay you now,' Ace admitted.

'Forget it,' Johnny said.

'I always pay a debt,' Ace said. 'Come back to the house with me.'

They walked to Ace's house in the rain.

'Want to play double or quits?' Ace offered.

'What's the bet?' Johnny asked.

'Anything you like. How about the last letter of the licence plate of the next car round the corner? You take first and I'll take second.'

'You're on,' Johnny said. 'Highest wins.'

The next car round the corner was an *R* reg. The one after it was a *P*.

'That's twenty quid I owe you,' Ace said.

'Double or quits again,' Johnny suggested. He wanted Ace's friendship, not his money. If they kept going, Ace was bound to double through. Then neither of them would owe the other.

'You choose the bet this time,' Ace said.

This was silly, Johnny thought. Anything would do. He pointed at a car window.

'Choose a drip at the top of the windscreen. First one to the bottom wins.'

'Nice one,' said Ace.

Each of them chose a drip of water. It was hard to keep track of each drip in the rain. Johnny's ran into another drip and shot down the screen.

'You win,' Ace said.

'No, that doesn't count. Play again.'

Ace shook his head. 'I can't afford to lose any more. We're here now. I'll get my dad to write you a cheque. It won't be the first time.'

Johnny didn't know what to do. He wanted to meet Vic Black, but not this way. Outside the house, he saw Mrs Black getting into her BMW.

'That's it, I've had enough!' she shouted. Then she drove off at speed.

In the driveway stood Ace's dad. Vic

Black looked a mess. His eyes were baggy. He was unshaven and wore only tracksuit bottoms. There was a removal van in the drive. Two men were carrying out a big leather sofa.

'What's going on?' Ace asked his dad.

'The building society is taking the house, son. I haven't been making the payments.'

'But where are we going to live?'

'We'll stay with your gran,' Vic said. 'I'm having the furniture put into storage. Don't worry. Now get upstairs and start packing.'

Ace looked at Johnny for a moment, then turned away. Johnny didn't know what to say. Vic Black looked totally wasted. He hadn't even noticed that Johnny was there.

Ace joined Johnny. 'Sorry,' was all he said.

'Why did your mum leave?' Johnny asked.

'Same reason my real mum left,' said Ace. 'Dad likes to bet. Sometimes he gets in a mess and drags the rest of us in. Looks like I'm going away for a while. I'll post that money on.'

'Forget it,' Johnny said. 'There's no need.'

Ace hurried into the house after his dad. Johnny walked home, thinking about Vic. Why did Ace gamble, when he saw what it did to his dad? Was it some kind of sickness? Was it in the family? Like father, like son?

Johnny thought about the last six months. He'd spent it all either playing or thinking about poker. Not girls or sport or school. Just poker.

Next day, Johnny didn't show up for the

game. Rajesh from Year Nine came looking for him.

'What's the matter?' Rajesh asked. 'You ill?'

'I've had enough,' Johnny told him. 'I'm all played out. Card games are a waste of time.'

'But you make a fortune from poker,' Rajesh said. 'What's the sense in stopping?'

'I never played for the money,' Johnny said. 'Money's just the way you keep score. I played because I enjoyed it, because I like to win.'

The poker game kept going, as Johnny had guessed it would. It kept getting bigger, even though Ace and Johnny weren't there. Johnny would join in now and then, when he had nothing better to do. Some days he won. Some days he lost. Pretty soon, however, he stopped going.

Several weeks later, two twenty pound notes arrived in the post. There was a short note with them. The note said *Be lucky*. It was signed *Ace*.